A BEE IN MY BONNET

Written by Barrie Wade
Illustrated by Jan Lewis

Collins Educational
An Imprint of HarperCollinsPublishers

Today Dad said
he could eat a horse.

Grandad said
he had a frog in his throat.

Aunty Mabel said
it was raining cats and dogs.

Grandma said
Andy had ants in his pants.

But when Mum said
I was getting her goat...

I got a flea in my ear...

14

and a bee in my bonnet.

Protect
the
Animals